JUNIOR FUN FAX ™

Make Your Own

Papier Mâché Models

Written by Brenda Apsley
Illustrated by Helen Marsden

Papier-mâché

Papier-mâché (say it pap-E-A mash-A) means 'chewed paper'. It has been used for over 2,000 years, and you can use it to make all sorts of things!

Making papier-mâché can be messy, so before you begin:

* Cover the area you are going to work in with old newspapers.

* Wear an apron. Make one from a plastic bin liner, with holes cut for your head and arms.

Remember

* Wallpaper paste will wash out of clothes.

* Peel off papier-mâché from clothes AFTER it has dried.

You'll need:

* Waste paper. Old newspapers are ideal, but you can use old telephone books, computer print out paper, etc. The thinner the paper, the smoother the object will be. Do not use glossy paper.
* A small packet of non-toxic cold water wallpaper paste.
* An old plastic bucket or washing-up bowl to mix the paste in.

Here are some more things you will find useful:
* scissors
* balloons
* modelling clay
* masking tape
* paints
* paint brushes
* a craft knife - and an adult to use it for you
* petroleum jelly or cooking oil
* a wire cake rack
* waste cardboard
* varnish

To make your own paste, ask a grown-up to help you mix 1 cup flour and 4 cups water.

Stir to get rid of lumps, then add 20 cups water which has just boiled. Boil in a big pan for 2-3 minutes until thick.

Read pages 2 to 9 carefully before trying to make any of the models.

Layering and Pulping

There are two main ways of making things with papier-mâché.

Layering

Strips of paper are pasted one on top of the other over a base or mould.

1. Tear newspaper into strips DOWN the page. For most models strips about 6cm wide and 20cm long are ideal. Always tear the paper. NEVER cut with scissors, as this will give your models hard edges. Tear lots of paper at once and keep the strips in an old cardboard box or carrier bag.

2. Mix HALF the paste following the instructions on the packet.

Pulping

Small pieces of paper are soaked in water, squeezed almost dry, then used like modelling clay.

1. Tear newspaper into lots of small 2-3cm squares. Put them into a bucket and pour on enough warm water to cover them.

2. Leave the paper for 24 hours, when it will have gone all mushy. This is paper pulp.

3. Add some mixed paste until the pulp stiffens and feels like soft clay.

Moulding is layering paper over a shape - a mould.

Good moulds should be smooth, rounded shapes like:
* blown-up balloons
* footballs
* plastic bowls
* large plastic bottles
* washing-up liquid bottles

Always:

1. Cover the mould with cooking oil or petroleum jelly. This will help you to pull your objects off or out of the mould easily.

2. Add strips of paper to cover the outside of the mould. EITHER dip each strip in paste, OR lay the strips in place then 'paint' paste over them, using a paint brush.

3. Let the strips of paper overlap slightly. For strength, lay one strip across, then one down, like this:

4. Add more paper strips until the mould is covered.

5. Add more layers of paper. You need at least six or seven layers to make a good strong object. Leave the edge ragged and uneven - you can trim it later with scissors.

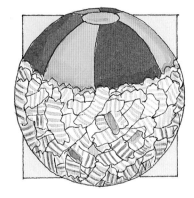

6. Leave to dry. A warm place where the air is moving is ideal. Put the objects on a wire cake rack so that air can get all around them.

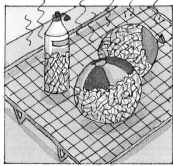

Drying will take about three days. Be patient - if papier-mâché is not REALLY dry it may fall apart.

7. When the papier-mâché is dry, CAREFULLY ease it off or out of the mould.

Decoration

When the papier-mâché is dry, always paint on a base coat. Paint the inside and outside with white emulsion paint. Two coats are best.

Plan your design on scrap paper before you begin drawing or painting. Mark outlines on the white emulsion paint in pencil.

Paint on your design. Use poster, watercolour or gloss paint. Dry between colours.

Add paper shapes. Cut out or tear shapes from gift wrap, magazines, catalogues, wallpaper, tissue paper, blotting paper, foil, sweet wrappers or cellophane, etc. Paste in place.

Protect papier-mâché models with varnish. Paint on at least two coats. Use gloss varnish for shine, or matt for a flat finish. The more coats of varnish you put on, the better the finished models will look.

Ideas:

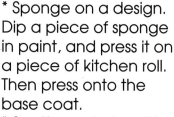

* Use wax crayons, pastels, felt-tips or marker pens.
* Trace designs from books and magazines.
* Potato-print small images onto flat objects.

* Make a raised design using string, cord, seeds, shells, beads, leaves, etc., painted over.

* Try zigzags, dots and simple shapes if you can't draw.

* Sponge on a design. Dip a piece of sponge in paint, and press it on a piece of kitchen roll. Then press onto the base coat.
* Spatter a design. Dip an old toothbrush in paint, and pull a piece of card across the bristles towards you. Let go. Use one colour or lots.

* Cut out a simple stencil image and sponge through it.

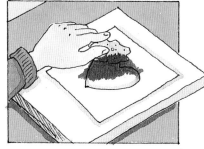

Bowls

You can make bowls in all sizes, depending on your mould. This one uses a balloon mould. Plastic bowls make good moulds, too. Layer the paper strips on the inside.

You'll need:
balloon
paper
paste
card
paints, etc.

2. Add six layers of paper strips and paste. Cover the bottom half of the balloon.

1. Blow up a round balloon. Keep the neck at the top.

3. When the bowl is REALLY dry, pop the balloon.
4. Leave the edge rough and `frilly', or cut it using scissors.

Base

Bowls need a base so that they will stand up. Cut out a long strip of card 2-3cm wide. Make a ring and sit the bowl in it. Hold in place with masking tape and layer over it.

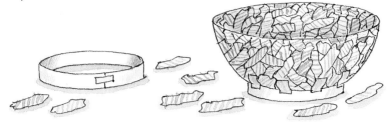

Lid

Mould around saucers or plates. Choose a size to fit your bowl. Add a handle.

Ideas:

* Paint the bowl blue and add a torn tissue paper orange goldfish.
* Leave a frilly top edge and paint like sunflower petals.
* Paint on a honeycomb design and add bees.
* Make a fruit bowl with painted fruit shapes.
* Join two bowls with masking tape for a butterfly bowl.
* Glue cord or string around the rim of the bowl. Paint over it.

Badges

Papier-mâché badges are very quick and easy to make.

You'll need:
card · tiny paper strips · paste · paints, etc.

1. Cut out a badge shape in card. Cereal packet card is fine.

2. Layer tiny strips of paper on one side. Cover the edges but leave the back flat.

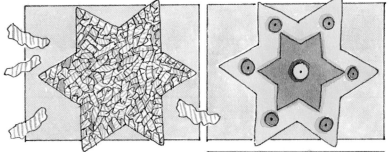

3. Dry and decorate.
4. Tape a large safety pin to the back.

Ideas:

* Choose simple shapes like circles, squares, rectangles, moons, stars, etc.

* Decorate a round badge for a birthday as a cake with candles. Use a sticky tab to stick it to a card.

* Glue a length of thin gift tie ribbon to the back of a balloon or kite badge. Make the kite string curl by pulling it across a scissor blade.

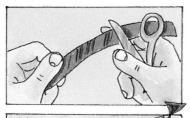

* Decorate a round badge as a rosette and add ribbons at the bottom.

* Add raised shapes using pulp.

* Make a large fish tank badge and fill it with gold foil fish.

* Make message badges using cut out letters from newspaper headlines. Paste in place before varnishing.

* Cut out bold letter shaped badges and wear a set to spell out your name.

* Make big bold number badges as birthday gifts.

Masks

You'll need:
oval balloon· paper strips · paste · string paints, etc.

1. Blow up the balloon.
2. With the neck of the balloon at the base, add features like noses.

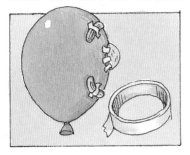

3. Cover the front half of the balloon with six layers of paper and paste.

4. When dry, pop the balloon and decorate.

For features:
* Use pulp or rolls of paper for eyebrows and noses.
* Make a nose from an egg box cup.

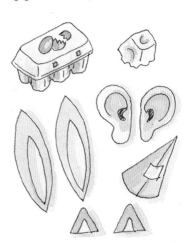

* For a long pointed nose, roll card into a cone.
* Cut out card ears.
* Use rolls of tissue paper or pulp for monster spots and bumps!

Decorate:
* Draw on eyebrows, spots, freckles, and scars.
* Sad white-face clown (Pierrot) masks look good hung on the walls.
* Paint on animal markings using books as a guide.
* Glue on extras like a wool-strip lion's mane, pipe cleaner cat's whiskers, or a curly moustache. Try toothpick whiskers and paper curl hair.
* Varnish.

Eye holes
Try on the mask. Ask a grown-up to mark where the eye holes should be, and to cut them out.

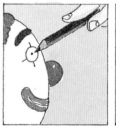

Ties
Ask a grown-up to make a hole at each side of the mask with a skewer or scissor blade. Knot a piece of ribbon or string through each hole. Tie in a bow at the back of your head.

Fishes and Parrots

You'll need:
scrap card · paper · paste · sticks · paints

Fish
1. Cut two fish shapes from card. Keep the outline smooth and simple, like the ones here.

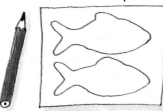

2. Put strips of masking tape around the edge to fix the two shapes together.
3. Pack dry scrumpled newspaper into the middle to make a fat fish shape. Add a final piece of masking tape.
4. Cover the fish with at least six layers of papier-mâché.

5. When dry, decorate using bright tropical-fish colours. Add markings like scales, gills, etc.
6. Use three coats of gloss varnish to give a really shiny 'fresh out of water' finish.

Ideas:
* Add pulp or button eyes glued in place.

* When painted and varnished, overlap rings of tissue paper to make 'scales', or use shiny sequins.

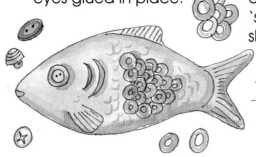

* Use sticky tabs to hang fish on your bedroom wall.
* Push a painted garden stick up into the fish and 'plant' in plant pots.

Parrots
Make parrots in the same way. Add a few real feathers after varnishing.

* Tie cotton to top fins and tie to a metal coat hanger to make a mobile.

Finger Puppets

1. Make some tubes of card about 6cm high. Try them on your fingers. Tape in place.
2. Layer over the tubes as usual, but use tiny strips of paper about 1cm x 3cm.
3. Use pulp to make heads.
4. Dry and decorate.

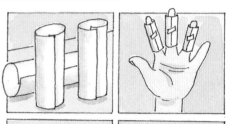

Ideas:

* Make bigger heads by pushing the tubes into ping pong balls and layering over them.
*Add hats made from card circles with a hole cut in the middle.
*For animals, make card wings, beaks, etc.
*Curled paper makes good feathers. Pull it across a scissor blade.

 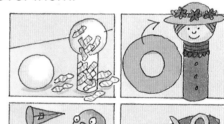

* Use a fine felt-tip pen to add eyes, etc.
*Add cotton or wool scraps for hair, beards, etc.

Finger Puppet Theatre

You'll need:
cereal box · paper · paste · paints, etc.

1. Cut a rectangle in the front of a cereal box. Tape the top flaps. Take off the bottom flaps.
2. Layer, dry and paint on scenery, curtains, etc.
3. Push finger puppets up on to the 'stage'.

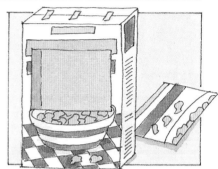

Put on a show like: Cinderella, with some VERY ugly sisters with bumps and cotton wool hair; Punch and Judy, plus Toby the dog, a crocodile and a string of sausages!; three fat brown bears and Goldilocks with yellow-wool hair; Little Red Riding Hood with a red paper 'cloak'; the Three Little Pigs with curly pipe-cleaner tails.

Bangles and Beads

You'll need: washing-up liquid bottle · card tube from kitchen or toilet roll · paper · paste · milk bottle

Bangles

1. Cut a 'slice' from a washing-up liquid bottle about 4-5cm wide. Use this as your mould.
2. For a rounded shape, scrunch a tissue into a sausage shape and tape in place. Layer with paper.

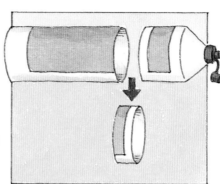

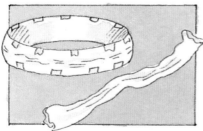

3. Add pulp jewel shapes, or glue on old beads, buttons or pasta shapes and mould over them.
4. Dry and decorate.

Ideas:

* Paint with metallic silver or gold paint.
* Paint 'jewels' in rich colours like emerald green and ruby red.
* Add texture by gluing string or twine around the bangle.

Curly bangle

1. Pull apart the kitchen roll card tube along the seam. This is the shape you should get:

2. Keep it open by wrapping it around a milk bottle. Make sure it is big enough to go over your hand.
3. Add five or six layers of paper.
5. Dry on the bottle.
6. Decorate. This kind of bangle looks good painted like a snake.

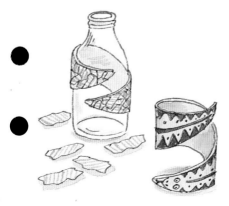

Beads

You'll need:
knitting needle or skewer · pulp · paints

1. Cover a knitting needle or skewer with petroleum jelly or oil.
2. Mould paper pulp around the needle into round or oval bead shapes.

3. Dry and decorate.
4. Thread on to thin elastic and tie to make necklaces and bracelets.

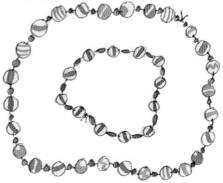

Sitting Cats and Lazy Tigers

You'll need:
washing-up liquid bottle · paper · paste .
sand or small stones · card · paint

Sitting Cat
1. Pour some sand or small stones into the bottle.
2. Use a ball of scrunched-up paper, taped in place, to make a head. Or mould a head using pulp.
3. Tape on card ears.

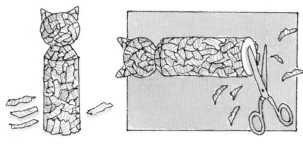

4. Cover the cat with 5 or 6 layers of paper strips. Dry.
5. Trim the base with scissors.
6. Decorate with paints, adding cat-like markings, eyes, etc. After varnishing, you could add some fuse-wire whiskers.

Ideas:
* Make a dog or lion model in the same way.
* Fill sitting cats with sand and use a matching pair as bookends, or a single one as a doorstop.

Lazy Tiger
1. Put some sand or small stones in the washing-up liquid bottle.

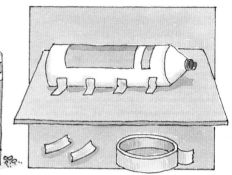

2. Lay the bottle on its side on a piece of card to make a base. Tape in place.

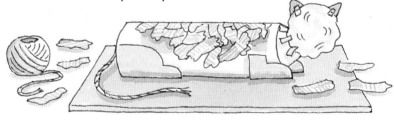

3. Add paper or pulp head and legs, and a string tail.
4. Layer, dry and decorate.

Idea:
* Make other lying animals, like cows, lions and dogs.

A World Globe

1. Blow up the balloon. With the neck of the balloon sticking out at the top, cover it with at least five layers of papier-mâché. Sit it in a plant pot or wastepaper bin to make it easier to handle.

2. Use pulp to add continents and islands. Use an atlas as a guide.

3. Dry and decorate. Keep the balloon knot at the top, where the Arctic will be. Do NOT pop the balloon. Paint seas blue, polar areas white, deserts yellow and land areas green and brown. Use an atlas as a guide. Draw in the equator using a felt-tip pen.

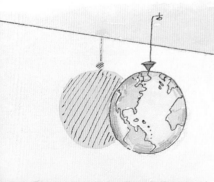

4. Tie a piece of cotton to the balloon neck and pin it to your bedroom ceiling.

Ideas:

* Paint pictures of endangered animals in their countries, e.g. pandas in China, elephants in India and Africa.

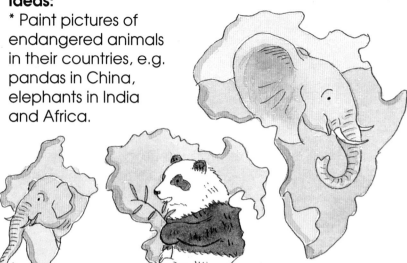

* Use pulp to mould craters and seas to make a model of the moon.
* Decorate small models as planets. Look in books for the right colours. You could hang the planets of the solar system from a wire coat hanger to make a mobile for your room.

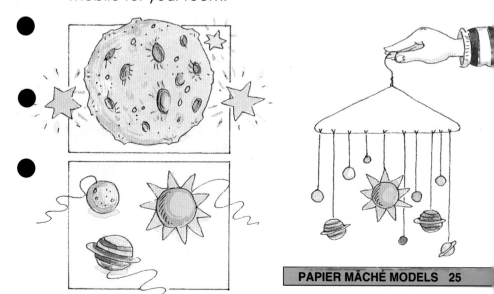

Piggy Bank

1. Blow up a small round or oval balloon. Keep the balloon knot where the piggy's tail will be.

2. Sit the piggy body on four toothpaste tube lids as legs. Tape in place. Tape on a paper snout. Add folded card ears like the ones shown here:

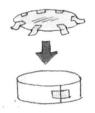

3. Layer paper over the piggy. Give the body at least 6 layers, but the ears about 3, so they will flop over.

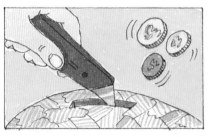

4. When dry, pop the balloon and ask a grown-up to cut a slit in the piggy's back, using a craft knife. This slit is for your money!

5. Base paint the piggy, then colour him pink, with black eyes and nostrils, etc.

6. Paint a pipe cleaner pink. Curl it and push it into the hole where the balloon knot was, to make a curly piggy tail.

Ideas:

* Make a cow, sheep or even a horse bank.
* If you want a really big piggy bank, use a HUGE balloon. Use egg box 'cups' for the legs and snout.

Round shaker

You'll need:
balloon · sand or dried beans · paper
paste · paints

1. Blow up a small round balloon and
cover with five layers of papier-mâché.
Layer up to the
balloon knot.

2. When dry, pop the balloon and pour some dried
peas or lentils through the hole. Fill it with different
things to make different sounds - try rice, sand,
small marbles, etc.

3. Seal the hole with a
strip of masking tape.

4. Base paint, decorate
(musical notes look
good) and varnish.

Tube shaker

You'll need:
kitchen or toilet roll card inner tube · dried peas or beans · paper · paste · paints

1. Tape up one end of the card tube and put some dried beans, peas or beads inside. Tape the other end.
2. Cover with layers of paper, dry and decorate.

Drum

You'll need:
a round mould · paper · paste · paints

1. Layer paper around the middle and over the top of your biscuit tin mould. Leave the bottom paper-free - you'll be taking the tin out later. Remember to cover the mould with petroleum jelly or oil!
2. Dry, decorate and varnish. Hit the drum with chopsticks or wooden spoon handles.

Hats and Crowns

Hat

1. Cut out a strip of card 10 -13cm wide. Make it into a circle and try on your head. When it fits your head well, fix in place with tape.

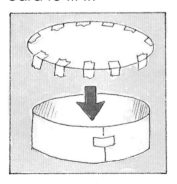

2. Measure across the hat. Cut out a circle of card to fit it.

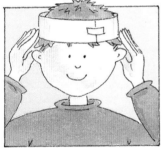

3. Tape the circle to the strip.

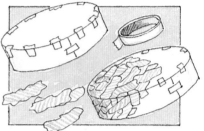

4. Add six layers of paper. Dry.
5. Paint, decorate and varnish.

Ideas:
* Add a card peak or brim before layering.

* Add pulp flowers, berries, etc.
* Glue on thick string around the edge before painting.
* Glue on feathers.

Crown

1. Cut out a long card band about 15cm wide. Fit it around your head and tape in place.
2. Cut the top edge into a 'crown' design.
3. Layer, dry, decorate and varnish.

Ideas:

* Use metallic paints.
* Glue on wine gum or Smartie 'jewels'.
* Mould big gems using pulp, and paint in jewel colours.
* White sequins make good diamonds; rice grains make good pearls.
* Glue on dried peas, etc. and paint as small gems.

Shallow plant pots, basins, balloons and plastic bowls all make good hat moulds. Try them on for size first!

More Ideas

Make Easter eggs for spring time. Mould modelling clay into an egg shape. Oil and layer. When dry, ask a grown-up to cut the egg in half along its length. Ease out the clay. Measure around the INSIDE of one egg half. Cut a 1cm wide strip of card and glue it in place so that 0.5cm shows. Now the two egg halves will fit together. Fill with mini chocolate eggs. Or make a bird's nest model and fill it with papier-mâché eggs, mini chocolate eggs - or baby birds.

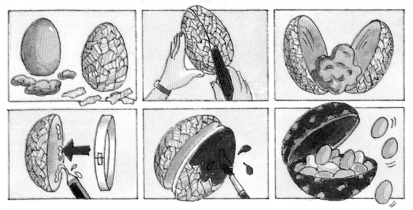

In summer use shells as moulds. Big shells like scallops and oysters work best. Layer on big shells. Use pulp on small ones. Decorate. Look in books for the right colours.

For Halloween, make a big fat pumpkin. Paint it bright orange and add black eyes, nose and mouth.

Make Christmas decorations for the tree. Cut out simple card shapes like bells, stars or holly leaves, and layer. Use a skewer to put holes in the top. Decorate and hang from the tree on loops or ribbon.